AF221138

Blockchain Technology - The Next Big Thing

Introduction To A Technology That May Change The World

Sebastian Merz

Bibliografische Information der Deutschen Nationalbibliothek:

Die Deutsche Nationalbibliothek verzeichnet diese Publikation in der Deutschen Nationalbibliografie; detaillierte bibliografische Daten sind im Internet über http://dnb.dnb.de abrufbar.

Herstellung und Verlag: BoD – Books on Demand, Norderstedt

ISBN: 978-3-7526-5896-5

Introduction

By using this book, you accept this disclaimer in full.

No advice

The book contains information. The information is not advice and should not be treated as such.

No representations or warranties

To the maximum extent permitted by applicable law and subject to section below, we exclude all representations, warranties, undertakings and guarantees relating to the book.

Without prejudice to the generality of the foregoing paragraph, we do not represent, warrant, undertake or guarantee:

- that the information in the book is correct, accurate, complete or non-misleading.

- that the use of the guidance in the book will lead to any particular outcome or result.

Limitations and exclusions of liability

The limitations and exclusions of liability set out in this section and elsewhere in this disclaimer: are subject to section 6 below; and govern all liabilities arising under the disclaimer or in relation to the book, including liabilities arising in contract, in tort (including negligence) and for breach of statutory duty.

We will not be liable to you in respect of any losses arising out of any event or events beyond our reasonable control.

We will not be liable to you in respect of any business losses, including without limitation loss of or damage to profits, income, revenue, use, production, anticipated savings, business, contracts, commercial opportunities or goodwill.

We will not be liable to you in respect of any loss or corruption of any data, database or software.

We will not be liable to you in respect of any special, indirect or consequential loss or damage.

Exceptions

Nothing in this disclaimer shall: limit or exclude our liability for death or personal injury resulting from negligence; limit or exclude our liability for fraud or fraudulent misrepresentation; limit any of our liabilities in any way that is not permitted under applicable law; or exclude any of our liabilities that may not be excluded under applicable law.

Severability

If a section of this disclaimer is determined by any court or other competent authority to be unlawful and/or unenforceable, the other sections of this disclaimer continue in effect.

If any unlawful and/or unenforceable section would be lawful or enforceable if part of it were deleted, that part will be deemed to be deleted, and the rest of the section will continue in effect.

Law and jurisdiction

This disclaimer will be governed by and construed in accordance with Swiss law, and any disputes relating to this disclaimer will be subject to the exclusive jurisdiction of the courts of Switzerland.

Inhaltsverzeichnis

BLOCK CHAIN

Blockchain, mostly known as the backbone technology behind Bitcoin, is one of the hottest and most intriguing technologies currently in the market. Since 2013 Google searches for "blockchain" have risen 1900%. Similar to the rising of the internet, blockchain has the potential to truly disrupt multiple industries and make processes more democratic, secure, transparent, and efficient. Entrepreneurs, startup companies, investors, global organizations and governments have all identified blockchain as a revolutionary technology. What are the most important benefits & challenges associated with the implementation of blockchain technology?

WHAT IS THE BLOCK CHAIN

The block chain is an online decentralised public ledger of all digital transactions that have taken place. It is digital currency's equivalent of a high street bank's ledger that records transactions between two parties.

Just as our modern banking system couldn't function without the means to record the exchanges of fiat currency between individuals, so too could a digital network not function without the trust that comes from the ability to accurately record the exchange of digital currency between parties.

It is decentralised in the sense that, unlike a traditional bank which is the sole holder of an electronic master ledger of its account holder's savings the block chain ledger is shared among all members of the network and is not subject to the terms and conditions of any particular financial institution or country.

If market hype is any indication, blockchain — the underlying technology for cryptocurrencies such as Bitcoin — is poised to solve multiple challenges facing the banking industry by enabling faster, secure and more transparent transactions. Yet the story of blockchain is one of unintended consequences.

Blockchain technology, was originally created as a tracking database for Bitcoin transactions. It was developed in 2009 to enable individuals and organizations to process transactions without the need for a central bank or other intermediary, using complex algorithms and consensus to verify transactions. Fast-forward seven years, and an array of startups and established technology, banking and finance players today are betting on blockchain to pro-vide a reliable alternative to systems that depend on intermediaries and third-party validation of transactions. Their goal is to leverage blockchain's distributed ledger approach to create a system that decentralizes trust — a radical departure from existing transaction processing methods — to significantly slash all types of transaction fees and reduce processing times.

The disruptive potential of blockchain is widely claimed to equal that of the early commercial Internet. A crucial difference, however, is that while the Internet enables the exchange of data, blockchain could enable the exchange of value; that is, it could enable users to carry out trade and commerce across the globe without the need for payment processors, custodians and settlement and reconciliation entities.

Although blockchain is posited as an open system for transaction processing across the financial system, banks are looking inward, experimenting with the distributed ledger approach to create efficiencies and a single version of digital truth.

Their goal is to automate processes, reduce data storage costs, minimize data duplication and enhance data security.

Similar to the Internet and e-commerce, an open-to-all blockchain that disrupts the tra-ditional financial market might only result from trial-and-error deployments within limited parameters, whether through internal trials or partnerships between incumbents and startups. However, to realize the full potential of blockchain across the financial system, the banking industry will need to come together and set standards that enable interoperability. That said, banks planning to deploy blockchains need to answer a series of fundamental questions. For example, given that existing systems are built on reliable legacy solutions, how will they deter-mine which process to move to a blockchain? Fur-ther, given blockchain's fast-changing landscape, it is critical to develop a thoughtful, long-term plan of action (e.g., experimenting, strategically deploying and then scaling in a logical progression) to ensure a successful transition from centralized legacy to fully distributed digital transaction processing.

The key considerations for banks exploring blockchain include:

- Identifying opportunities for innovation.

- Determining feasibility and impact on existing systems.

- Testing proofs of concept.

- Understanding the regulatory and data security implications.

- Dissecting the blockchain implementation: open vs. permissioned.

- Planning for transaction scalability.

- Forming partnerships and cross-functional and cross-industry collaboration.

- Risk reduction through data integrity ensured by chronological storing of data enforced with cryptography. This, in turn, reduces the compliance burden and cuts regulatory costs in areas such as know your customer (KYC) initiatives.

WHY IS THIS PREFERABLE TO OUR CURRENT BANKING SYS-TEM?

A decentralised monetary network ensures that, by sitting outside of the evermore connected current financial infrastructure one can mitigate the risks of being part of it when things go wrong. The 3 main risks of a centralised monetary system that were highlighted as a result of the 2008 financial crisis are credit, liquidity and operational failure. In the US alone since 2008 there have been 504 bank failures due to insolvency, there being 157 in 2010 alone. Typically such a collapse does not jeopardize account holder's savings due to federal/national backing and insurance for the first few hundred thousand dollars/pounds, the banks assets usually being absorbed by another financial institution but the impact of the collapse can cause uncertainty and short-term issues with accessing funds. Since a decentralised system like the Bitcoin network is not dependent on a bank to facilitate the transfer of funds between 2 parties but rather relies on its tens of thousands of users to authorise transactions it is more resilient to such failures, it having as many backups as there are members of the network to ensure transactions continue to be authorised in the event of one member of the network 'collapsing' (see below).

A bank need not fail however to impact on savers, operational I.T. failures such as those that recently stopped RBS and Lloyds' customers accessing their accounts for weeks can impact on one's ability to withdraw savings, these being a result of a 30-40 year old legacy I.T. infrastructure that is groaning under the strain of keeping up with the growth of customer spending and a lack of investment in general. A decentralised system is not reliant on this kind of infrastructure, it instead being based on the combined processing power of its tens of thousands of users which ensures the ability to scale up as necessary, a fault in any part of the system not causing the network to grind to a halt.

Liquidity is a final real risk of centralised systems, in 2001 Argentine banks froze accounts and introduced capital controls as a result of their debt crisis, Spanish banks in 2012 changed their small print to allow them to block withdrawals over a certain amount and Cypriot banks briefly froze customer accounts and used up to 10% of individual's savings to help pay off the National Debt.

As Jacob Kirkegaard, an economist at the Peterson Institute for International Economics told the New York Times on the Cyrpiot example, "What the deal reflects is that being an unsecured or even secured depositor in euro area banks is not as safe as it used to be." In a decentralised system payment takes place without a bank facilitating and authorising the transaction, payments only being validated by the network where there are sufficient funds, there being no 3rd party to stop a transaction, misappropriate it or devalue the amount one holds.

BITCOIN

Bitcoin is on the rise as a digital currency used worldwide. It is a type of money controlled and stored entirely by computers spread across the Internet. More people and more businesses are starting to utilize it.

Unlike a plain U.S. dollar or Euro, bitcoin is also a form of payment system sort of like Paypal or a credit card network.

You can hold on to it, spend it or trade it. It can be moved around cheaply and easily almost like sending an email.

Bitcoin allows you to create transactions without revealing your identity. Yet the system operates in plain public view.

Anyone can view these transactions which are recorded online. This transparency can drive a new trust in the economy. It even resulted in the downfall of an illegal drug ring, discovered shuffling funds utilizing bitcoin and shut down by the U.S. Government.

In many ways bitcoin is more than just a currency. It's a re-engineering of international finance. It can dissolve barriers between countries and frees currency from the control of federal governments. However it still relies on the U.S. dollar for its value.

The technology behind this is interesting to say the least. Bitcoin is controlled by open source software. It operates according to the laws of mathematics, and by the people who collectively oversee this software. The software runs on thousands of machines worldwide, but it can be changed. Changes can only occur however when the majority of those overseeing the software agree to it.

The bitcoin software system was built by computer programmers around five years ago and released onto the Internet. It was designed to run across a large network of machines called bitcoin miners. Anyone on earth could operate one of these machines.

This distributed software generated the new currency, creating a small number of bitcoins. Basically, bitcoins are just long digital addresses and balances, stored in an online ledger called the "blockchain." But the system design enabled the currency to slowly expand, and to encourage bitcoin miners to keep the system itself growing.

When the system creates new bitcoins it gives them to the miners. Miners keep track of all the bitcoin transactions and add them to the blockchain ledger. In exchange, they get the privilege of awarding themselves a few extra bitcoins. Right now, 25 bitcoins are paid out to the world's miners about six times per hour. Those rates can change over time.

Miners watch bitcoin trades through electronic keys. The keys work in conjunction with a complicated email address. If they don't add up a miner can reject the transaction.

Back in the day, you could do bitcoin mining on your home PC. But as the price of bitcoins has shot up, the mining game has morphed into a bit of a space-race. Professional players, custom-designed hardware, and rapidly expanding processing power have all jumped on board.

Today, all of the computers vying for those 25 bitcoins perform 5 quintillion mathematical calculations per second. To put it in perspective, that's about 150 times as many mathematical operations as the world's most powerful supercomputer.

And mining can be pretty risky. Companies that build these custom machines typically charge you for the hardware upfront, and every day you wait for delivery is a day when it becomes harder to mine bitcoins. That reduces the amount of money you can earn.

Why do these bitcoins have value? It's pretty simple. They've evolved into something that a lot of people want and they're in limited supply. Though the system continues to crank out bitcoins, this will stop when it reaches 21 million, which was designed to happen in about the year 2140.

Bitcoin has fascinated many in the tech community. However, if you follow the stock market, you know the value of a bitcoin can fluctuate greatly. It originally sold for $13 around the early part of 2013. Since then it has hit $900 and continues to move up and down wildly on a daily basis.

The real future of bitcoin depends much more than on the views of a few investors. In a recent interview on reddit, Cameron Winklevoss one of the twins involved in the Facebook lawsuit with Mark Zuckerberg and an avid bitcoin investor, predicted that one bitcoin could reach a value of $40,000. That is ten times what it is today.

A more realistic view suggests that speculators will eventually cause bitcoin to crash. It does not incorporate the ability to utilize its currency in the retail environment, seemingly a must for long term success. Its wild fluctuations also make it a huge risk for investment purposes.

Still bitcoin pushes the boundaries of technology innovation. Much like Paypal in its infancy, the marketplace will have to decide if the risk associated with this type of digital currency and payment system makes for good long term business sense.

Characteristics of Bitcoin

Bitcoin has the characteristics of traditional currencies such as purchasing power, and investment applications using online trading instruments. It works just like conventional money, only in the sense that it can only exist in the digital world.

One of its unique attributes that cannot be matched by fiat currency is that it is decentralized. The currency does not run under a governing body or an institution, which means it cannot be controlled by these entities, giving users full ownership of their bitcoins.

Moreover, transactions occur with the use of Bitcoin addresses, which are not linked to any names, addresses, or any personal information asked for by traditional payment systems.

Every single Bitcoin transaction is stored in a ledger anyone can access, this is called the blockchain. If a user has a publicly used address, its information is shared for everyone to see, without its user's information of course.

Accounts are easy to create, unlike conventional banks that requests for countless information, which may put its users in jeopardy due to the frauds and schemes surrounding the system.

Furthermore, Bitcoin transactions fees will always be small in number. Apart from near-instant completion of processing, no fees are known to be significant enough to put a dent on one's account.

The road that lays ahead of Bitcoin

In a world of accelerated technological changes, it would be unwise to predict what tomorrow may bring. There are many factors that may come into play in the evolution of Bitcoin. If it will run into severe obstacles, it will rapidly be displaced by another crypto currency that will overcome the obstacles. In the contrary case, the network effect will carry Bitcoin to dominance. Whether or not it's Bitcoin, crypto currencies are here to stay as an intriguing concept and a groundbreaking technology.

Statutory and regulatory frameworks in some countries are stacking against Bitcoin, yet there is no evidence so far to think that Bitcoin could not coexist alongside other fiat monetary systems. In fact, they may address different market needs and even complement each other synergistically, like the coexistence of commodity money and fiat money.

Another factor that mustn't be disregarded is that Bitcoin is an early stage technology, where millions of dollars constantly exchange hands, making it a dream target for faceless international hackers, hostile intelligence services, or just about any group of hippie coders.

BENEFITS OF BLOCKCHAIN TECHNOLOGY

1. Disintermediation & trustless exchange

Two parties are able to make an exchange without the oversight or intermediation of a third party, strongly reducing or even eliminating counterparty risk.

2. Empowered users

Users are in control of all their information and transactions.

3. High quality data

Blockchain data is complete, consistent, timely, accurate, and widely available.

4. Durability, reliability, and longevity

Due to the decentralized networks, blockchain does not have a central point of failure and is better able to withstand malicious attacks.

5. Process integrity

Users can trust that transactions will be executed exactly as the protocol commands removing the need for a trusted third party.

6. Transparency and immutability

Changes to public blockchains are publicly viewable by all parties creating transparency, and all transactions are immutable, meaning they cannot be altered or deleted.

7. Ecosystem simplification

With all transactions being added to a single public ledger, it reduces the clutter and complications of multiple ledgers.

8. Faster transactions

Interbank transactions can potentially take days for clearing and final settlement, especially outside of working hours. Blockchain transactions can reduce transaction times to minutes and are processed 24/7.

9. Lower transaction costs

By eliminating third party intermediaries and overhead costs for exchanging assets, blockchains have the potential to greatly reduce transaction fees.

CHALLENGES OF BLOCK-CHAIN TECHNOLOGY

1. Nascent technology

Resolving challenges such as transaction speed, the verification process, and data limits will be crucial in making blockchain widely applicable.

2. Uncertain regulatory status

Because modern currencies have always been created and regulated by national governments, blockchain and Bitcoin face a hurdle in widespread adoption by pre-existing financialinstitutions if its government regulation status remains unsettled.

3. Large energy consumption

The Bitcoin blockchain network's miners are attempting 450 thousand trillion solutions per second in efforts to validate transactions, using substantial amounts of computer power.

4. Control, security, and privacy

While solutions exist, including private or permissioned blockchains and strong encryption, there are still cyber security concerns that need to be addressed before the general public will entrust their personal data to a blockchain solution.

5. Integration concerns

Blockchain applications offer solutions that require significant changes to, or complete replacement of, existing systems. In order to make the switch, companies must strategize the transition.

6. Cultural adoption

Blockchain represents a complete shift to a decentralized network which requires the buy-in of its users and operators.

7. Cost

Blockchain offers tremendous savings in transaction costs and time but the high initial capital costs could be a deterrent.

The Bank of England's recent report on payment technologies and digital currencies regarded the blockchain technology that enables digital currencies a 'genuine technological innovation' which could have far reaching implications for the financial industry.

How does the block chain work?

When an individual makes a digital transaction, paying another user 1 Bitcoin for example, a message comprised of 3 components is created; a reference to a previous record of information proving the buyer has the funds to make the payment, the address of the digital wallet of the recipient into which the payment will be made and the amount to pay. Any conditions on the transaction that the buyer may set are finally added and the message is 'stamped' with the buyer's digital signature. The digital signature is comprised of a public and a private 'key' or code, the message is encrypted automatically with the private 'key' and then sent to the network for verification, only the buyer's public key being able to decrypt the message.

This verification process is designed to ensure that the destabilising effect of 'double spend' which is a risk in digital currency networks does not occur. Double spend is where John gives George £1 and then goes on to give Ringo the same £1 as well (Paul hasn't needed to borrow £1 for a few years). This may seem incongruous with our current banking system and indeed, the physical act of an exchange of fiat currency stops John giving away the same £1 twice but when dealing with digital currencies which are mere data and where there exists the ability to copy or edit information relatively easily, the risk of 1 unit of digital currency being cloned and used to make multiple 1 Bitcoin payments is a real one. The ability to do this would destroy any trust in the network and render it worthless.

"What the deal reflects is that being an unsecured or even secured depositor in euro area banks is not as safe as it used to be."

To ensure the system is not abused the network takes each message automatically created by a buyer and combines several of these into a 'block' and presents them to network volunteers or 'miners' to verify. Miners compete with each other to be the first to validate a block's authenticity, specialist software on home computers automatically seeking to verify digital signatures and ensure that the components of a transaction message logically flow from the one preceding it that was used in its creation and that it in turn reflects the block preceding it that was used in its creation and so on and so forth. Should the sum of the preceding components of a block not equal the whole then it is likely that an unintended change was made to a block and it can be stopped from being authorised. A typical block takes 10 minutes to validate and therefore for a transaction to go through though this can be sped up by the buyer adding a small 'tip' to encourage miners to validate their request more quickly, the miner solving the block 'puzzle' being rewarded with 25 Bitcoins plus any 'tips', thus is new currency released into circulation, this incentivisation ensuring that volunteers continue to maintain the network's integrity.

By allowing anyone to check a proposed change against the ledger and validate it the block chain removes the need for a central authority like a bank to manage this. By removing this middleman from the equation a host of savings in terms of prescribed transaction fees, processing times and limits on how much and to whom a transaction can be made can be negated.

Sounds too good to be true.

It is, every type of system has its own particular risks, a decentralised one being no different. The main threat to Bitcoin's decentralised network is the '51% threat', 51% referring to the amount of the network's total miners working collaboratively in a mining 'pool' to validate transactions. Due to it becoming more costly in terms of time and processing power for an individual to successfully validate a transaction as a result of the network becoming bigger and more mature individual miners are now joining 'pools' where they combine their processing power to ensure a smaller but more regular and consistent return. In theory, should a pool grow large enough to comprise of 51% or more of total network users it would have the ability to validate massive double spend transactions or refuse to validate authentic transactions en mass, effectively destroying trust in the network. While there is more incentive built into the system to lawfully mine Bitcoin than destroy it through fraud the 51% threat represents a risk to such a decentralised system. To date mining pools are taking a responsible approach to this issue and voluntary steps are being taken to restrict monopolies forming, it being in everyone's interests to maintain a stable system that can be trusted.

So... despite this risk the Bank of England likes the thing that sounds like it could put them out of business?

The BoE are looking beyond Bitcoin and digital currency payments specifically and envisioning ways that the block chain can make existing financial products and platforms more efficient and add value to them. One needs only to look at existing financial assets such as stocks, loans or derivatives which are already digitised but which sit on centralised networks to appreciate the opportunities that exist for the individual by removing the middleman...

... and becoming your own stockbroker. Coloured Coins is a project that aims to allow anyone to turn any of their assets or property into something they can trade.

Think 'The Antiques Roadshow'. I love that show, especially when a little ol' dear finds that she's been using a 14th Century Ming dish worth £200,000 to keep fruit in on her sideboard. Coloured Coins would allow the owner of the dish (or their car or house) to have one or more of their Bitcoins represent a part or whole of the value of their asset so that they could be traded in exchange for other goods and services, a single Bitcoin holding a value of the entire £200,000 or they issuing 200 coins each with a value of £1000.

Similarly, a business could issue shares represented by digital currency directly to the public which could in turn then be traded without the need for an expensive IPO or traditional stock exchange and shareholders could vote using a secure system similar to how transaction messages are currently created. Patrick Byrne, CEO of one of the

US's largest retailers which was the 1st major on-line retailer to accept international Bitcoin payments is currently exploring plans to create such a stock exchange powered by the block chain which he hopes will negate current inherent problems such as 'abusive naked short selling' where traders can sell shares they don't own which drives down share prices and which was felt contributed to the fall of Lehman Brothers.

The digitising of assets could also revolution-ise the crowdfunding industry. Kickstarter is an example of a platform that facilitates the funding of products by micro-payments from interested members, often in return for small mementos upon completion of the project such as signed merchandise or a copy of one of the first products to be produced. With the ability to easily digitise an asset and issue shares in it and all future profits for example investors may be more inclined to invest more heavily.

And speaking of crowdfunding... Vitalik Buterin recently raised £15m in crowd-sourced funding for his Ethereum Project which he believes will represent the future of the block chain. The project supports numerous programming languages so as to allow developers to build online products and services like social media, search or chat forums as alternatives to those run by corporations like Google, Facebook and Twitter. "You can write anything that you would be able to write on a server and put it on to the blockchain," Buterin told Wired. "Instead of Javascript making calls to the server, you would be making calls to the blockchain." Currently a community of 200 users are building voting apps, domain name registrars, crowd-sourcing platforms and computer games to run on Ethereum, 'ethers' mined through the maintenance of the platform by volunteers being required for this.

THE FUTURE OF BLOCKCHAIN

The potential of the block chain to improve the way we communicate, bank, manage our assets etc is huge and only limited by the imagination of people like Vitalik Buterin and the Ethereum community and the willingness of current institutions to change.

The future of finance could be dominated by blockchain technologies. A traceable global currency complete with an efficient infrastructure will not only result in massive cost reduction for all market participants, it will change global banking. Bitcoin will do for payments what email did for communication.

What is changing?

- Blockchain will be adopted by central banks and cryptographically secured currencies will become widely used.

- Nasdaq will launch blockchain-enabled digital ledger technology that will be used to expand and enhance the equity management capabilities offered by its Nasdaq Private Market platform.

- The settlement of currency, equity and fixed income trades almost instantaneously through permissioned distributed ledgers creates a significant opportunity for banks to drive efficiency and potentially create new asset classes.

Control

- New technologies such as blockchain have the potential to reduce cyber risks by offering identity authentication through a visible ledger.

- There is no reason why requirements for numbering, maintaining and indexing records and communicating information provided in records could not be met through an electronic ledger system.

- Car rental agencies could use smart contracts that automatically allow rentals when payment's received and insurance information is confirmed through a blockchain record.

- A refrigerator equipped with sensors and connected to the Internet could use blockchain to manage automated interactions with the external world-anything from ordering and paying for food to arranging for its own software upgrades and tracking its warranty.

- Small businesses could use blockchain to create trusted trading platforms among themselves.

- Blockchain could potentially help bring robustness and transparency to the post-trade environment.

- New technologies such as blockchain have the potential to reduce cyber risks by offering identity authentication through a visible ledger.

- A bank could pay the supplier instantly over the Internet.

- Blockchain technology will alter timing on risk.

Crime

- A new blockchain startup has claimed its software could help track down criminals faster and cheaper than ever.

- Connecticut are warning parents that a new Darknet cryptocurrency called Bitcoin could be to blame for helping underage drinkers to get buzzed.

Implications

Banks.

- Blockchain will be adopted by central banks and cryptographically secured currencies will become widely used.

- Blockchain could replace central banks.

- Real risks remain for banks that choose to get involved with cryptocurrency firms.

- Blockchain technology could reduce the UBS's infrastructure costs in cross-border payments, securities trading and regulatory compliance by as much as $20 billion a year by 2022.

- The number of applications within and outside the banks could be reduced as the Blockchain transaction contains all relevant information for the successful transfer of assets and/or related contracts.

- Deutsche bank's economist sees blockchain as a threat because of the lack of the IT infrastructure to support the technology involved.

- Ethereum is much more general purpose than bitcoin and could be useful for banks.

- The future of finance in many nations could be dominated by Bitcoin and cryptocurrencies.

- A private blockchain run by banks could end up as just "another cartel" and function as poorly as the payments consortium.

- Banks could become the "custodians of cryptographic keys".

- The blockchain could save lenders up to $20 billion annually in settlement.

- Blockchain technology could be used to bypass today's centralised financial infrastructure entirely.

Industries

- Time and education will need to play a role as other industries are just realizing one of the core innovations of the blockchain is its ability to reduce or eliminate trusted counterparties in the transaction process.

- Blockchain has the potential to create new industry opportunities and disrupt existing technologies and processes.

- Blockchain technology will make the world even smaller as it increases the speed and efficiency of transactional activity.

Governments

- The future of finance in many nations could be dominated by Bitcoin and cryptocurrencies.

- Blockchain technology could be used to distribute social welfare in developing nations.

- Elections are currently an expensive and arduous. Thanks to blockchain tech they will soon be instantaneous.

The blockchain really could change the world, making financial crises much less damaging and reducing frictions in global commerce. It could also fade into the relative obscurity of narrowly conceived technical innovation. The technology deserves to be properly explored.

Regulators can make the difference by giving it some space.
